Gliders and Sliders

Written by Jo Windsor

Some animals have found
different ways to move.
They can glide.
And they can slide.

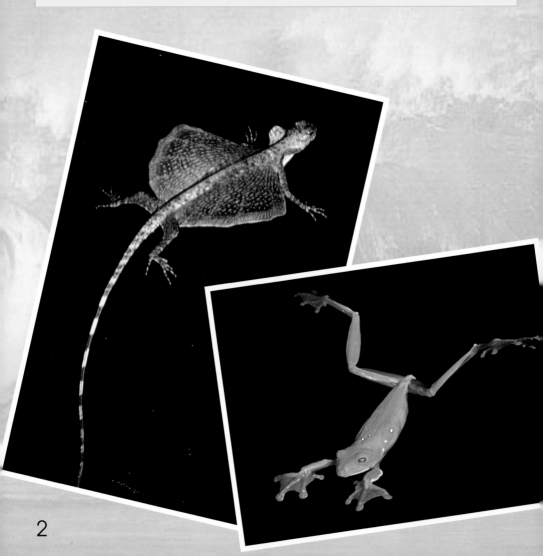

3

This animal can glide.
It is a flying squirrel.
It can stretch out
its front and back legs.
It can glide from tree to tree.

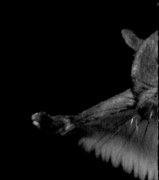

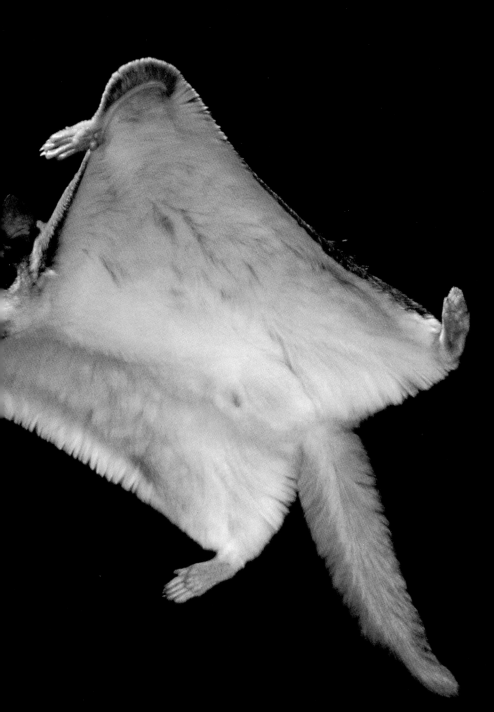

This lizard can glide.
It jumps into the air
and glides from tree to tree.

This frog can glide, too.
It stretches out its toes
and glides in the air.

People like to glide in the air.
These people are in a plane
called a glider.
It will glide in the air
and land on the ground.

These people are
in hang-gliders.
They can glide in the air
and land on the ground.

Some animals have found
different ways to move
on the ice.
They can slide.

Penguins move across the ice
by walking and sliding.
It is faster for the penguins
to slide.

This seal can slide, too.
It slides across the ice
and into the hole.

People can slide
on the ice and snow, too.
They slide on
skis and toboggans.

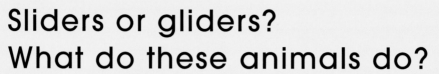

Sliders or gliders?
What do these animals do?

Index

Guide Notes

Title: Gliders and Sliders
Stage: Early (4) – Green

Genre: Non-fiction
Approach: Guided Reading
Processes: Thinking Critically, Exploring Language, Processing Information
Visual Focus: Photographs (static images), Index
Word Count: 181

THINKING CRITICALLY
(sample questions)
- What do you think this book is going to tell us?
- What animals do you see on the front cover? How do you think these animals move?
- Focus the children's attention on the index. Ask: "What animals and things are you going to find out about in this book?"
- If you want to find out about penguins, what page would you look on?
- What are you going to find out about on page 4?
- If you want to find out about hang-gliders, what page would you look on?
- Look at pages 2 and 3. How do these animals move?
- Look at pages 8 and 9. What are these people using to move?

EXPLORING LANGUAGE

Terminology
Title, cover, illustrations, photographs, author, illustrator, photographers

Vocabulary
Interest words: glide, slide, stretch, toboggan
High-frequency words: called, or

Print Conventions
Capital letter for sentence beginnings, full stops, commas, question marks